Don't

Give

Up!

God Is Not Through with You Yet

The spiritual Truth By

Bill Tolbert

WESTBOW·
PRESS
A DIVISION OF THOMAS NELSON
& ZONDERVAN

Scripture taken from the King James Version of the Bible.

WestBow Press books may be ordered through booksellers or by contacting:

WestBow Press
A Division of Thomas Nelson & Zondervan
1663 Liberty Drive
Bloomington, IN 47403
www.westbowpress.com
1 (866) 928-1240

ISBN: 978-1-4908-2910-4 (sc)
ISBN: 978-1-4908-2911-1 (e)

Library of Congress Control Number: 2014904191

Printed in the United States of America.

WestBow Press rev. date: 03/07/2014

CONTENTS

INTRODUCTION

He that overcometh shall inherit all things; and I will be
his God, and he shall be my son (Revelation 21:7)

Writing this book was an opportunity for me to find healing. I must admit as I revisited my past I became intensely emotional. It is heartbreaking keeping a secret like this without anyone to talk to. This grief caused my life to become unbearable at times. The Holy Spirit guided me to write this book. One reason was so that I would be healed, and the second was so that I would be able to help the next person dealing with similar struggles. The true essence of life is when you understand that once you are strengthen, it is your job to strengthen others.

A child is given away by his mother at the tender age of three months old. Initially he lives with his grandparents, but his childhood with them is chaotic because he is never able to live with both of them at the same time. His grandparents had separated, and are not living together anymore. When it is time to start first grade he moves in with his uncle and his wife, who lives in Chicago. He lives with them until adulthood. However, he finds living without a mother or a father invited struggles and adversities, and these hardships followed him into his adult life. This memoir will allow the reader to realize that life is simply not about the struggle and the abuse he or she may encounter, but it is more about the courage and the ability to never give up. The answer instead is to put the past behind and to move forward. This is my story. I am addicted to it and now it is time to let it go! For I declare, "I am an appointment not an accident!"

My mother had plans of putting me up for adoption when I was born, but my grandfather stepped in and stopped her. She had already given up one child before I was born for adoption, a baby girl. So, my grandfather told my mother that he would raise me. Many years later I remember seeing my birth certificate, typed on it as the last name was baby boy *Smith*, and handwritten was my first name *Billy*. My name was handwritten because I believe that my mother had no plans to keep me. In the place where the father's name was listed, typed was *"legally omitted."* Another revelation was to learn the actual date of my birthday, which is so important for a child. It is sad to say that none of the adults in my life took time to find out my real birthday. As long as I remember, I was told my birthday was October 26, 1957 only to discover that my birthday was actually October 28, 1957. I was sixteen or seventeen applying for my first job, before I found this out.

For me, forgiving others often started as a decision of surrendering my will to God; I could no longer respond to life based on my short-sighted perception. This surrender invited God to begin working anew in my life on a deeper level, thereby allowing Him to heal me. To forgive does not mean that you excuse the deed or the person; neither does it provide God's forgiveness for their actions against you; only God can do that. While nothing can undo the past, we can do something about the circumstance of our present and future. Sometimes, it is necessary to go through trials and tribulations to receive your reward. My passion has led me into my purpose, which is to tell my story. My expectation is to help a child that felt as I once did; a child that believes he or she has no hope; a child that believes no one loves them; a child that believes he or she can do nothing to change their life. The reality is that they do not have to GRIEVE over what they did not receive; what did or did not happen to them; or how they were treated; or who did not love them; or how they were raised. *But, I want them to know that there is hope; just don't give up! God is not though with them yet!*

THE BEGINNING

And we know that all things work together for good to them that love God, to them who are the called according to His purpose.

(Romans 8:28)

As a toddler I thought that my grandmother was my mother, because I was raised to call her *Big Mama*. I can remember a time that really sticks out in my memory, when I was living at Big Mama's house. I was playing outside and I ran after a marble into a main street, I was almost hit by a truck. Thankfully the truck barely touched me but it left a mark on my face. The truck driver stopped to see if I was alright, he ask me where did I live and took me home to Big Mama. I will always cherish this, because it was one of those moments when I felt loved and cared for. The following day when I took my kindergarten pictures at school, you could see the bruise near my eye. I was so proud of that picture, it meant a lot to me. There were times when I went to church with Big Mama; I would see my three aunts singing in the choir. Big Mama would cry, and I would always ask her why was she crying. As I look back I thought maybe she was thinking about my mother and wishing she was there too.

My granddaddy lived in a small kitchenette apartment. When I went to visit/live him, I slept on the couch and we had to use the bathroom down the hall. There was one bathroom on each floor and we lived in the basement. My granddaddy had a girlfriend and he insisted that I call her grandmamma, so I did. Granddaddy and his girlfriend lived together, and their relationship was very tumultuous. They drank heavily and fought all the time. The important thing though is what has always stuck out in my adult life is that my granddaddy worked every day until he retired. Granddaddy would always fight Lucy when they got drunk. One particular time when I was there someone called the police. The police arrested the both of them, and took me to jail also. Another time, granddaddy got more drunk than usual; I guess he must have been mad with Lucy about something. Usually when he was in this condition he was very generous, so I asked him to buy me a soda pop. He put his money in the hallway pop machine, but nothing came out. He became so angry that he broke his hand on the pop machine. I don't know why this stand out in my mind, but it just does.

I lived with my granddaddy most of the time. In the small kitchenette, we all slept in the same room. I was on the couch, and he and Lucy slept in their bed. I was five or six years old when granddaddy felt that I was getting too old to sleep in the same room as he and Lucy. This living situation prompted him to find somewhere else for me to live. So he asked my Uncle LC if he paid him ten dollars a week would he let me live with him. LC was my mother's brother. My uncle said yes.

I was the oldest child living in my uncle's home. There were a total of ten of us by the time I had made eighteen. As a young child I had no concept of understanding that I did not have parents. Since I had not started school yet I pretty much depended on television to understand family relationships. However, when I started attending school, and hearing the other kids talk about their parents, then my mind would start to wonder why I did not have a mother and father.

GOD WHY ME? -
WHY NOT ME?

For as many as are led by the Spirit of God, they are the sons of God.
For ye have not received the spirit of bondage again to fear; but ye
have received the Spirit of adoption, whereby we cry, Abba, Father.
(Romans 8:14-15) And because ye are sons, God hath sent forth the Spirit
of his Son into your hearts, crying, Abba, Father. (Galatians 4: 6)

By the time I was ten years old looking back over my life
I believe I had the understanding of accepting Jesus into my
life, and believing that God existed. However, not many of my
family members went to church, except for my grandmother.
When I was an adolescent I would go to different churches with
neighbors and friends. As I moved into my teen years, I turned
away from my faith. Though I still acknowledged the existence
of God, I decided that he did not fix things well enough in my
life. Therefore, I would sometimes find myself angry with God.
There were so many times that I would just lie in bed and cry.
I was in so much emotional pain that I couldn't get out of bed.
It would be years later that I would ask God again to help me,
and when I did that, it was as if a weight had been lifted off
me. My childhood was such an intensely emotional experience
that I knew there had to be something more for me. There were
times I could literally feel the power and presence of God. One
of the biggest lessons that God had to teach me was that he loves

me. This was quite significant because as a child, I didn't feel loved at all. This doesn't mean that I don't still have challenges, heartaches and disappointments; what it means is that I am sure of one thing: God is real and He will always be there for me simply because I am his beloved child.

It was implied that I should leave the past behind and not worry about what happen to me as I was growing up. But not to worry, or think about the difficulties hurled at me only hurt more, because I felt like I needed to know God, why me? !Yes, it is a fact that life goes on, but I never thought there could be a better life than the pain that I was going through at that time. I did not understand that life should have been different. I thought that was how things were supposed to be. I was supposed to be angry; I was supposed to be sad; I was supposed to be scared all the time. Now God has positioned me to help other people who are experiencing what I went through. And I say again "God why not me?!"

Even though I was never physically imprisoned, I often felt mentally imprisoned. I was living behind a imaginary fence, which was intended to guard me, but that same fence became my personal penitentiary. As a young adult I was plagued by the fact that my mother never wanted me and I desperately needed to know why. I could not understand why after giving me up, my mother had three other children. The older I became, the more questions I asked. I want to know specifically why my mother gave me away. I could not help feeling that she never loved me. Why was I so unworthy and why were my other siblings more important to her than me? When I asked, her response was that she could not afford to take care of me. This explanation was somewhat plausible, but I always thought in the back of my mind, why did she have three more children and never attempted to get me back. As I grew up I would always ask God why me, and once I became an adult I would still ask God why me? The Holy Spirit revealed "why not me?" God has a work for me to do, and for His work I have to go through something. "I am an appointment not an accident."

TROUBLE IN MY WAY

I waited patiently for the Lord; he turned to me and heard my cry.

He lifted me out of the slimy pit, out of the mud and mire; he set

my feet on a rock and gave me a firm place to stand. He put a new

song in my mouth, hymn of praise to our God... (Psalm 40:1-3)

I can remember being made to call my uncle "da-da" and his wife "ma-ma." This upset me somewhat because I never considered them a substitute for my parents.

When my uncle would leave for work I was disciplined by his wife. She would tell me how dumb I was, and I that I would never amount to anything. It seemed that she would say this to me every day—day in and day out (an expression I often heard grownup's say). I found myself crying often as a little boy because I could not understand why I was being treated this way. What had I done, not to have my own mother and father? When I entered first grade learning was a difficult task for me. It seemed academic comprehension was beyond my reach. I had problems learning the alphabet and counting numbers. My uncle wife often rewarded me with a whipping for not learning. I had to sit at a portable black board for hours at a time each day until I learned the alphabet, how to read and how to count. My uncle wife constant physical and verbal abuse became so traumatic that sometimes I would urinate on myself, and then get whipped for that. I couldn't win!

7

Somehow I passed on to the next grade level. I don't know why, because my grades were horrible, and I felt I was not learning anything, at least not as I should have been. During this difficult time not only was I being disciplined at home for not learning, but I would also be discipline at school from some of my teachers. Between the two, I was so traumatized that I was afraid to go to school and afraid to go home. My spelling tests were especially difficult, because if you did not get a passing grade the teacher was allowed to punish you with a spanking. I really hated when report cards were issued, because that meant an automatic whipping at home. Back in the 1970's it was nothing to come to school with whips all over your body; people would just say he or she must to have gotten a whipping last night. No one ever questioned the bruises, not even a higher authority.

There were times in school when we had what we would call *show-and-tell* (this is when you brought your favorite toy from home and talked about it). The other children would always talk about what their mother and father brought them, and I would have to stand up in class and say I got my show and tell from my uncle and aunt. I found out later that my grandfather was buying most of the things I would get for Christmas and many of my things such as clothing and school supplies were donated to me from the school. The items my family gave me were always the hand-me-downs; growing up it was very seldom I would receive anything that was brand new. When I came to my uncle's house, there were already two children there. One was his step-daughter and the other was his son, After I arrived it seemed that my uncle wife had a baby almost every year. By the time I left at eighteen there were ten of us. During the years my uncle would also take in other cousins, and they would live with us temporarily however, everyone would eventually go back home to their mothers, except for me. So that is when I really became curious about why was I there and begin to ask questions. Sometimes I would over hear adults talking about me, but at my age I couldn't understand what it all meant. When I was very young living with my uncle, most of the time I was kept away from the rest of my mother's side of the family. When my grandmother passed, I was not allowed at her funeral. I never found out if it was my age, or if they were just keeping me from the family. When I first moved in with my uncle and his family, there were some good times because I really did not know what was going on. In 1964 we lived in the projects on 37th street in Chicago, Illinois. I attended the Doolittle School. One day being very rebellious I was in the closet playing with matches and there was a nylon dress with a long belt on it. The belt caught on fire and I accidently set the whole bedroom on fire. The fire department was called but I cannot remember if they ever found out that I set that fire.

Looking back now, I do not believe that my uncle wife ever liked me; I can remember her only being nice to me when my uncle was around. She always told me how dumb I was, how I would never amount to anything and that is why my mother did not want me. She even told me that when I was an infant, I cried a lot. My aunt had a habit of often pinching me when no one was looking. She did not realize, or maybe she did, how much the things she said and did hurt me. I was always crying and did not understand why. I believe my uncle also resented my presence at his home, because he often whipped me without explaining why. I don't think I was actually bad, but it seemed like this was the only time I received his attention. I was so young and did not understand how much I was starving for affection. I looked for it from almost anyone. I don't ever remember being shown any kind of love. It would be really difficult when I saw other children shown love by their parents or other family members.

I did not realize that I was missing a motherly bond, but as I look back every female adult I came across I felt some kind of bond and desired their comfort. I was heavily affected when it came to my female school teachers, because often this was the only time I received any degree of attention and affection. My attachment to these motherly role models became so bad that at the end of the school year when I had to change teachers, I would always cry because I did not want to leave. If I had a new female teacher the next school year, this cycle would start all over again. This repeated itself until I was about in the eighth grade.

I developed a passion for drawing to keep my mind off of the abuse. I would love to draw cartoon characters, and I had become very artistic. I would sometime spend my time creating one drawing after another; it's amazing that my so call family never said anything about my talent. It was something they could finally say something good about, but instead my aunt would tear up my drawings if she felt that I was somehow being disobedient to her. I cannot describe how devastated I felt by her actions.

I was about eight or nine years old when my family moved to another project on the south side of Chicago. Even though we changed location the mistreatment continued. I recall a specific event. My family had a cat, and my uncle and aunt were either too cheap to buy cat litter, or could not afford it. Therefore, I had to go outside, dig up dirt, put it in a box and carry it up stairs to our apartment for the cat. We also had a puppy, and it was also my responsibility to walk the dog. We lived on eighth floor; there was elevator but most of the time it was broke, so unfortunately I had to use the stairs. I went up and down the stairs all by myself; once I got outside I had to cross a busy street. This was a huge responsibility for me at the time. I would take the dog to a vacant lot where I always went to get the dirt for the kitty litter, and then walked the dog. On my way home one day the dog got away from me. He ran out into the busy street and was hit by a car. Unfortunately, the poor puppy died. When I returned home and explained what happened of course it was all my fault, and I received yet another whipping. No one considered how devastating it was for a young child to see that puppy die so tragically; add to that the tragedy of getting whipped for something that was out of my control. My uncle and his wife gave me a lot of responsibility since I was the oldest. I had to feed the younger children, change their diapers, and generally take care of them. Sometimes I was even left to babysit.

The abuse continued from both my uncle and his wife. My uncle did most of the whipping. In 1970 we moved again, this time to a house in a better neighborhood. We were still on the south side of Chicago, but this new place was about fifty blocks south of the projects. By then I was in the fifth grade and eleven years old. When we moved it was the middle of the school year. My uncle and his wife transferred their two children to the school near our new home. However, I had to continue to go to the same school. This meant that I had to ride public transportation, two buses, to and from school alone until the school year was over.

By this time I had become a very rebellious child. Because of the ongoing abuse, I remained a very scared and confused child. My fear of my uncle was overwhelming. I think I wet the bed until I was fourteen years old. Whipping me only aggravated the problem; it never helped me to stop. As I look back now, no one noticed the emotional trauma I was going through. It was so hard for me then; I did not know what it felt like to be given a hug and to be told that I was loved. I would sometime get hugs from my female teachers; as a child I was always longing for someone just to tell me they cared. I was so vulnerable at that time and was always looking for affection so much so that I began to trust the wrong people who would eventually take advantage of me. There were more times than I can remember that I would think of killing myself. I blamed myself for even being born, therefore, if I killed myself who would care anyway?

Later my granddaddy and girlfriend moved in with us. My granddaddy would try and show me love but I believe he just did not know how. It seemed that he understood what I was going through because there were many times he would get on my uncle and aunt about mistreating me. There were four boys in a bedroom, and they felt since I was the oldest it was my responsibility alone to keep the room clean. I also had to mop the kitchen floor every day, which was white. It seemed that the other kids began to catch on to how I was being treated. They would try to do the same, but I would try and get them back every chance I could. His wife taught them that they could hit me, but that I was not allowed to hit them back. Her reasoning was that since I was older I was not permitted to hit them back. They would do anything to provoke me; sometimes they would be very rude to me and call me names such as *stupid*. I learned to fake it and act as though it did not bother me. My uncle's wife became a thorn in my side because she would actually tell lies to my uncle just so he would whip me. He never questioned me about what his wife said that I had done.

One day I just got tired of being hit by the other kids. So one of her oldest sons, hit me and I went completely off on him right in front of his mother. I did not care anymore because I knew I was going to get whipped anyway. The flash backs are so vivid it is as if I am there again. I have been trying to work through my past but it is not easy. Sometimes I cannot sleep without thoughts of what they did to me flooding my mind.

When I was about fourteen or fifteen years old my aunt decided she was going to whip me herself while my uncle was gone for whatever reason. I decided to just let her hit me without crying this time. This really made her angry and I knew it, but I refused to cry no matter how hard she hit me. Well, when my uncle came home she told him that I would not cry, and he came in the room and beat me again. I cried and cried, not from him hitting me, because I was pretty much use to that, but it was because he listened only to her once again, and never were my thoughts or opinion considered. The pain I felt was internal rather than external.

We had a limited amount of food because there were so many mouths to feed. Often, I left the table hungry. Unfortunately, I picked up a habit of going to the corner grocery store every morning before school to steal food. I had gotten so slick at it that I tore holes in my pockets so I could hide the food I stole in my back. This way my pockets did not stick out. There were numerous times that the other kids and I would fight over who was going to get the food the adults left on their plates.

While in the seventh and eighth grades, I was constantly teased by the other kids in school because of how I dressed and smelled. They had a nick name for me, BB, which stood for Billy the Bum. The school system just pushed me through because my grades were always bad. My uncle's answer to that was to keep beating me, not considering for one moment that maybe there was a problem. I was told so much how dumb I was that I even started believing it myself. All my life no one ever took the time to find out what was wrong with me. There were many times in my life when I felt like I just wanted to die. I was in such misery that I often thought about killing myself. I thought about it more often when I became a teenager.

As a teenager I started making more friends at school. I did not care anymore if my uncle and aunt didn't care about me, or if my mother did not care about me. More and more I had come to a point where I did not care about myself either. Fortunately I found an outlet in sports, which for a while kept me occupied. The sport I was most interested in was basketball. When I was not on punishment, I was out doors as much as possible. This was my excuse for staying away from home as much as possible. I ended up playing several different sports because I had so much anger inside of me. The competitive aspect in sports help me relieve some of the aggravation I felt inside, it was my outlet. It would help me change my anger into something positive. The older I became, I invented more and more ways to stay away from home for longer and longer periods of time.

I recall a specific day when I was on punishment. It was a warmer day than usual on March 27, 1972. I went outside even though I was not supposed to. I snuck out the backdoor to go play strike out, a baseball game. Well, there was a shooting at the playground and I got shot with a ricochet bullet that hit me in the foot. I was admitted in the hospital because I needed surgery to remove the bullet. I stayed in the hospital almost a month. I actually had no problems with being in the hospital, because I was finally getting the affection and love from nurses that I was missing at home. Maybe once a week someone would visit me, usually my uncle's wife would visit. No one came on the days I had my two surgeries. I guess it was my uncle who made sure his wife came to visit me, because he never did. I found out years later that my mother knew I was in the hospital and she never visited me either.

In 1972 I graduated from eighth grade. I barely made it through. Even though I frequently ditched school, remarkably I did graduate! I was so proud of myself for graduating, and hoped that despite all the negative criticism my family would finally see that I accomplished something positive. Well, not one person showed up at my graduation, not even my mother. I had to come home from the graduation with the neighbors. I believe this was my first experience with alcohol because I was devastated that none of my family showed up at my graduation. I was fourteen years old, and I got so drunk on my graduation night that I was sick enough to throw up! The over indulgence in drinking continued on all through my teenage years. I was only getting drunk because I was feeling so sorry for myself. To make matters worse my uncle and his wife were drinking and fighting all the time. Their drinking became so bad that they were drinking everyday by the time I turned eighteen.

My uncle and his wife never gave me an allowance even though they were getting a check for me once a month (which I found out once I turn eighteen). To make money I would go around the neighborhood and ask for odd jobs. I was willing to do almost anything. I would cut grass, baby-sit, and go to the local store for the neighbors who could not go themselves. I painted houses, did my own fundraisers by selling flower seeds in the summer, and shoveling snow in the winter. My hands and feet would get frost bitten, because I was never properly dressed for the cold. By the eighth grade I had a paper route delivering newspapers. I had to get up before school at 5:00am in the morning no matter what the weather; in Chicago that could be rain, cold, sleet or snow. Since I was making my own money, I had to take the little money that I earned to buy my own school clothes, and anything else I needed. If I had any money left over my aunt and uncle would take it from me. Making my own money made me feel very proud of myself. I was finally able to buy something new instead of always wearing hand-me-downs!

I grew to highly resent my uncle and his wife. For one thing, I knew my aunt never liked me, but she always pretended she did when she was around other people. After I began high school, my aunt and uncle made me walk almost six miles to and from school nearly every day; their excuse was that they did not have the money to give me to ride the bus. However, when their oldest daughter graduated from eighth grade the following year, they were there for her graduation, and she got to ride the bus to the same school I attended. I was so frustrated at the unfairness of this instead of walking to school I went the opposite way. I also began to hang out every day with my friends after school. My uncle and aunt seemed not to care about me or anything that I did. Their attitude caused me to give up on myself as well. My behavior got worse and worse and I started speaking my mind regardless of the consequences. I had pretty much grown numb to the beatings. It was at this point that I decided to reach out to my mother, to try and find out if what I was told most of my childhood was true–that she did not want me.

CHASING AFTER MY DREAM

All bitterness, anger and wrath, insult and slander must be remove
from you, along with all wickedness. And be kind and compassionate
to one another, forgiving one another, just as God also forgave
you in Christ. (Ephesians 4:31-32)
With God's power working in us, God can do much, much
more than anything we can ask or imagine
(Ephesians 3:20).

I was about nine or ten years old I began to go visit my
mother. At the time she lived in a low income apartment in the
State Street Projects in Chicago. I usually saw her only two
or three times a year. Since I was younger, I don't remember
having a lot of questions. I was still very confused; no one really
explained to me why I was visiting my *so-called* family and then
had to always come back to my uncle and aunt. During these
visits with my mother I never remember her showing me any
love or affection. However, my sisters and brothers would try and
make me feel that they loved me. I often reminisce about playing
with my younger brother Charles during my visits; he initially
thought we were cousins. This became another painful memory,
because to me it was obvious that my mother never wanted me.
Going home after spending a weekend with my brother and
sisters was almost unbearable. I can only remember getting one
Christmas gift from my mother as a child that I know of.

At almost thirteen, the abuse was on-going, and I wanted to be around my mother more often. My aunt always asked me, "Why I wanted to go around someone who didn't care about me?" I internalized what I was hearing about my mother and how she felt about me. What have I done so wrong that my mother did not love or want me? By this time my mother had moved into a new house. It was still in Chicago, but it was in a nice south side neighborhood. To escape the environment at my uncle's house I asked to go to my mother's house more often. I actually learned how to catch the bus to her house on my own. Although my visits to my mother were more frequent, I could not dismiss my feelings of rejection. I tried to talk to my mother, and convey to her how I was being treated at my uncle's house. However, it seemed that she didn't care. At one time she told me that there was nothing she could do because they were my legal guardians. I felt like I had a hole in my heart. I started getting the feeling that it was true, my mother really did not care about me.

Therefore, I became angrier and rebellious. I was drinking more and getting into fights frequently, because I felt my own mother rejected me. Despite what I was feeling I was a very quiet person, although I was filled with rage. People were constantly picking on me and trying to provoke me to fight, and I usually gave in. I found that fighting was a way to release all my anger. Soon I would arrange for people to set up fights for me, which caused me to be in constant trouble. I stayed away from home as much possible. I began standing up to my uncle and telling him how I did not want to be there anymore.

All I remember is being told that I could not move away from home until I was 18 years old. One day I got so out of hand that uncle drove me to my mother, which was all I ever wanted. But, I was heartbroken again because she said, "I don't want him; take him back with you."

As a teenager I beat myself up all the time emotionally, wondering what had I done to deserve this, and why didn't my mother want me? Why did my uncle take me in, if he didn't care for me either? My abuse of alcohol started to increase. I drank so heavily that I would not only get drunk, but I had started having seizures. This happened so often that the doctors were trying to figure out why I was having so many seizures, and why was I drinking so much? As a result, I was admitted to a mental health hospital in the psychiatric ward. I stayed there about a week; they were trying to find out what was wrong with me. However, the doctors were unable to make a diagnosis for me, because how do you diagnose the need for attention and love?

As you know, my aunt and uncle had the tendency of bringing other children into our home. One summer, they brought home a girl who was a year younger than me. She was sixteen, and her name was Charlene. She began to show me attention and we eventually became intimate. We didn't consider ourselves a couple; but once again here was a female showing me that she cared for me. It was the attention I continuously craved. After that summer was over, she went back home and returned to school. I was hurt because in my mind here was another person who left me. I didn't want to go back to high school because as usual I had to walk. I found out that since I was over sixteen I could sign myself out of school and go to Job Corp. So to get out of that house that's what I did. I believed that no one cared whether I went to school or not. I dropped out of school and signed up for Job Corps in 1974. The day before I was to leave I received a phone call from Charlene. She said her mother was taking her to the doctor because she thought that she was pregnant. I still had to leave, so I packed up my small amount of clothes, and my uncle gave me bus fare to catch the bus downtown to leave for the Job Corps.

Once downtown, I felt so alone again. I had to catch the bus by myself. When I got there, I saw other families seeing their children off, kissing and crying. A week later I arrived at Job Corps in Indianapolis, Indiana. I spoke with Charlene and she confirmed that she was pregnant. I informed her that I was going to do whatever I had to do. In the meantime, her mother took her to my uncle and aunt and advised them that her daughter was pregnant. I do not know what was said, but I learned later that Charlene's mother put her out of the house. So she came to live with my uncle and aunt. From what I understand, aunt allowed her live there until she found out that I was returning home, and then she made Charlene leave. She did not want me and Charlene to be together. I looked forward to coming home and seeing the person who was carrying my baby. I dreamed of being there to see my child born. I kept telling myself that I was not going to let what happened to me happen to my baby. This is the first time that I had really thought about being a daddy.

When I got home Charlene was gone. I was told to never try to get in touch with her, because that was not "my baby". I decided not to go back to the Job Corps; I went AWOL. After all I had been through as a child, not having parents, now at seventeen, and expecting my own baby, all I could think of was that I was not about to let my child go without a dad. Charlene's mother permitted her to move back in there home. Charlene had the baby January 31, 1975. I was threatened that I was not to try to get in touch with her. So I walked around in a daze thinking of my child and how they were keeping me from her. Charlene named her Latosha. By this time I was driving, and since I had a license my uncle would sometimes let me use his car. I decided one day that I was going to see my child. Since both families kept me away from my new baby, being unable to call Charlene, she thought that I did not want to be bothered. Latosha was three months old. I had to sneak to Charlene's house. The visit went okay except that I brought my uncle and aunt oldest daughter along with me. I was able to explain to Charlene why she had not heard from me. I also found out that Charlene's mother was angry with me, because my uncle wife told her that I said Charlene's baby was not mine. Therefore, her mother said I was to never come to their house. Of course their daughter told my uncle and aunt where we had been. I can't remember what happened, but I do know that it was three years before I saw my child again.

I got my first real job at age 18. I began volunteering at one of the Chicago Public School in the cafeteria with uncle's wife. Actually, I had no choice. I was made to volunteer, which turned out to be good for me. His wife would make me get up every morning at 4:00a.m.and go with her to the school and volunteer. The cafeteria manager, Jean Brown, liked my independence and motivation to work; so she was the reason I was permanently hired. Now that I was 18 years old I was finally able to move out of my uncle and aunt house. I later discovered that the real reason why I could not move out. My uncle and aunt were receiving government assistance for me and it would end once I became eighteen years old if I was not in school. I always dreamed of leaving at eighteen, this started as early as thirteen years old. It all made sense to me now why so much emphasis was put on my eighteenth birthday, and also why my aunt and uncle tolerated me for so long. The money had something to do with it.

I moved out and lived with my sister Francine. Over the years I confided in her often, and explained to her what I was going through and how I wanted to leave my uncle and his wife's home because it never felt like a true home to me. Thankfully, she told me that once I made eighteen years old I could come and live with her. This arrangement started out great, but my uncle still had a hold on me, and I was afraid of him. The first few months after I left home, I was had to drive and pick my aunt up for work every day since we were working at the same place. I did this until I made up my mind one day that I was not going to do it anymore. As time passed, they were slowly becoming eradicated from my life. I felt a tremendous release from all of the years of abuse. When I was about 20 years old I decided that I was going to start calling him and his wife by their first names. I was made to call them *da-da and ma-ma*; I never felt they deserved those titles from me. As I got older I begin to feel more comfortable standing up to him, because I did not believe a child should be made to call anyone mother or father; that should be the child's choice. (I now have two step children, Bryan and Keanna that I raised, and I have never made them call me dad, but until this day I'm still dad to them and probably always will be.)

I stayed with my sister until her boyfriend and I could no longer get along. I came home from work one day, and my sister had moved out taking with her everything, except the items that belonged to me. I had no other choice but to ask my mother if I could move in with her. She reluctantly said I could move in with her, but I never knew that this move would open old wounds, and that I would be hurt all over again. Despite this, living with her was like a dream come true; it made me feel like I finally belonged and I hoped that she would finally love me as I loved her. I never knew if the love was there because she never gave me any physical or verbal clues that she loved me. Unfortunately, this living situation did not last very long. I felt more like a tenant, than a child moving back home. I felt that she never acknowledged my presence in the same ways she did my other siblings. We held small insignificant conversations periodically, but there were so many negative vibes, which made me feel as though she did not want me living with her. I felt as though she did not know who I was, and I did not know her either; the sad fact was that she was okay with this. At nineteen this was a difficult pill to swallow. I ultimately found my own place and lived with my child's mother. Regardless of my mother's inability to bond with me, I would spend as much time with her as possible, because I continued to seek her love and acceptance. Now, when I look back I believe that my mother just did not know how, or just did not care. There were times in my life when I thought that my mother hated me. I tried so hard to make her feel proud of me, and the more I tried, the more she rejected me. There were times that I felt like my mother was very threatened by our conversations. I continued to worry and ponder over what I had done for my mother not to want to have a relationship with me. Because of our broken relationship, I made a promise to myself that I would never treat my children this way.

I tried desperately to find my baby girl Latosha and thankfully I did. My baby was now three years old. I began to keep her on weekends so that she could get to know me. By this time I was expecting my second child; her name was Sherell. She was born in 1978. I tried to do a little better than I did with my first child, even though it was not my fault that I was not in her life. I was a young man who had never been taught how to love. I never really bonded with anyone, and no one ever showed me any kind of love except for my grandfather and grandmother. Therefore, I tried to be the best father that I could with my children, but I really just did not know how. I just know I never wanted my children to ever feel the way I did growing up.

I was determined to find someone to love me; I was emotionally starving for affection. As a young man I had many relationship problems. I was in constant need for someone to love me, to give me a hug, and to tell me that everything was going to be alright. I even tried turning to the neighborhood street gangs looking for the affection. All I needed was to be around people that truly believed in me. I remember when I got shot; it seemed that I got so much respect from my peers that I got even more involved in the gangs.

After my second child was born, I began to question my mother about my father. I felt like if she did not care for me maybe there was a dad out there who would care about me. I began to have problems understanding how to be a father, but the more I asked my mother about my father the worse our relationship became. She just did not want to talk about it. By this time I had pretty much given up on asking why she had given me up. I just started to accept it. I now wanted to know who my daddy was and how could I find him. When I was younger I asked my grandfather did he know who my dad was and all he could tell me is that he thinks that my dad played in a band. I went to other family members asking about my dad, my mother's sisters and brothers. At first they would not really talk, they would just say they did not know. But when I became a young adult I remember going to visit my Uncle Leon in Mississippi and I asked him did he know why it seemed that my mother hated me so much? He finally broke down and told me, Billy I really believe it's because you look like your dad so much, and he really hurt your mother. He believed that the older I got, the more I looked like my dad. He said that his name was Charles Tolbert and like my grandfather said, he can only remember that he played in a band and live in Gary, Indiana.

By now I was more confident that I wanted to find my dad, so I began questioning my mother every chance I got. Her only response was to ask me, "Why are you trying to find your dad. How do you know that he even wants to be bothered with you?" As time went on, we would have some very heated arguments about my dad and why she gave me up. It would get so bad that we would go months, and even years without talking to one another. My mother would become irritated even if I came around her. It would hurt me so bad; I just could not understand how a woman could carry a child for nine months and not have any feelings for that child. My mother always asked me why I could not just forget the past. For me, the greatest harm I experienced was her lack of reaction and protection. I had to deal with this all of my life. I did everything in my power to treat my children differently, but and it was difficult for me to show them love, because I never had it nor was I taught love. But I made it my business to always be in my children's life and try and give them something I always wanted and never had, and that was the love of a parent. Because I was taught that I was a failure at everything I did, I secretly thought I might be a failure at being a good father too. But, I felt that if I ever found my dad; he would be able to rescue me. Since I didn't have a dad growing up, I created the perfect image of what a father should be, and I tried to fulfill it.

SEXUAL ABUSE:
VICTIM WITHOUT A VOICE

But you Lord, are a shield about me, my glory,
and the lifter of my head (Psalm 3:3)

The incident of sexual abuse happened to me when I was 10 years old or younger; I don't want to get into too much detail about this. Sadly, I don't remember much about it; I tried to block it out of my memory. There were times when I tried to let my family know that something was wrong. I remember telling my aunt and uncle that I did not want to go to bed when one of my aunt's particular family member was over visiting and spending the night. I knew he would touch me inappropriately, and my reluctance to go to bed was the only way I could verbalize what was happening to me. He would always volunteer to sleep with me in one of the two bunk beds in our bedroom. I did not know how to say no; I was just terrified to go to sleep when he was over. He always said to me that if I told anyone, he was going to say that it was *me* touching him, and that *I* was going to get a whipping. (Looking back, I believe this family member saw that I was being mistreated and he took advantage of that.)

I did not fully comprehend what was really transpiring until I got older. At age sixteen I became very angry with my mother and my uncle for not being there for me. I felt that they were not there to protect me and if my mother was there I would have never gotten hurt. As I grew older I became extremely shy and quiet around people, even to this day I still get into that mood. As a survivor of child molestation I felt that there were so many obstacles to disclosing my sexual abuse. I was apprehensive that no one would believe me; I felt shameful and guilty. I blamed myself and was fearful of the retaliation.

Being a victim of sexual abuse almost took my life. In addition, because I was abuse by a male, there were times when I would feel sexually conflicted. As I became older the trauma affected me more and more. I developed a lot more anger, and I wanted to fight all the time to release that anger. Even if you don't talk about sexual abuse, it's going to come out in some way. For me, in addition to the aggressive anger, I drank excessively. I also became very promiscuous as a young adult. I feel that this too was in response to the trauma I endured. Child abuse is as close as you can come to murdering a child. I was dead emotionally because I was molested as a child, and even today I still feel very emotional about it. There were no lessons or discussions when I was growing up about safe touching, and what to do if someone approaches you in a sexual way. I now I realize that God allowed this to happen to me, so that I could educate and help other young people. I'm still freeing myself every day, and I want to tell other victims that it was never their fault. I was a victim for a long time, but now I am a survivor!

The abusers took away my power and control, and in return gave me disgrace, self-reproach, and a secret to keep at all cost, even at the cost of making me feel like a victim for the

29

rest of my life—until now. There were times when I thought of committing suicide. This emotional breakdown was because of the stress related to my abuse issues, and my belief that I was unloved. My lack of family nurturing and protection resulted in many failed relationships. One of my problems was that I fell in love too hard; all I wanted was to be loved by someone, and it was hard for me to except rejection. It took me a long time to form lasting relationships with women. I strongly believe it was due to the abuse I received as a child. Also, it was because I never had a positive male role model. The men in my life all dealt with problems in a negative way. I pretty much did what I saw other men do, except to hit women. Even though that was all I saw from my grandfather to my uncle, I made a promise to myself that I would never hit women. Because of my desperate desire for love and acceptance, I went through phases in my life when one woman was not enough. I had to have two or three at a time, but I found out later in life that this lifestyle was extremely stressful; I was always trying to be at three places at once. As an adult male I found that I had no self-esteem and was very licentious.

The people I should have been able to trust and turn to in times of need were often the very people who stole my trust and used my body for their own sick needs. I never tried to tell anyone, because there was no safe person to tell that I thought would believe me, and not put the blame on me. I felt so guilty about the abuse that I was ashamed to tell anyone. I believe that I hid the mental, physical, and sexual abuse so far down in the recesses of my mind that I now have no concise memory of the facts. However, I feel that all of the denying, blocking and minimizing had to end in order for me to get beyond the victim stage.

When Johnnie, my second wife, came into my life, I was still very promiscuous, but thanks to her prayers and understanding, I can say I'm finally free. A lot of it had to do with the love and respect that I have for her. She was the first person that I really felt comfortable telling about being sexually abused as a child. I guess I could say that she was part of my healing. I am very relieved to say that even though I was a victim, I never became a victimizer myself. Praise God! I would never steal innocence or purity, or consider tragically affecting a child for rest of his or her life. I am empowered to make my transformation from victim to survivor. Innocence and lost as a child is a sad thing; it takes a long time to heal. I now realize why today I still have serious issues with adults who molest children. The depth of pain and confusion that sexual abuse causes in young males must be arrested by helping them to seek help. We are re-victimizing these young African American men by not encouraging them to seek help. I wondered why me?

But there is a book by Pastor Jamal Bryant, and he said and I paraphrase, *that when trials happen to you in life, they build character.* God can't use you if nothing ever happens to you.

As a victim of sexual abuse, it was hard for me to trust people and make friends; it caused me to be a loner and to be looked upon as being awkward and strange to others. I suffered extreme self-extreme issues and found that I always doubted myself. Living with being molested may cause a multitude of social ills such as, depression, hate, anger, sexual disease, alcohol and drug abuse, prostitution, homosexuality, suicide, homelessness, prison, cold-heartedness, loneliness, nightmares, panic attacks, quitting, low self-confidence and low self-esteem. I have experienced a number of these conditions and would still be in a bad state, if it was not for deliverance through Jesus Christ. Through the Gospel of Jesus Christ I have changed my life and character. I am in my second marriage with five beautiful children and several grandchildren. I have been able to accomplish this with the help of the Lord on my side. My goal is to help other people who may be suffering because of physical and sexual abuse, but are afraid to speak out due to family threats and punishments. I would like to help others change their lives as I have changed mine. After reading through my experiences, I am hopeful that children and young adults will be encouraged to speak out against those who abused them, whether physically, emotionally or sexually. I think of the future leaders, scientists, mathematicians, engineers, evangelists, and teachers, who may never realize their true potential because of abuse from those they trust.

Getting to a point where people can express their need for help can be very challenging, especially when it involves the sexual abuse of a straight African American male in this country, or any other for that matter. It took me an extremely long time to get to the point where I no longer cared what other people thought of or about me in reference to something that I had absolutely no control over. I basically got tired of being tried. I knew that something was terribly wrong with me across the board, because of the things that I would or would not do in relationships. The vivid flashbacks, the lack of emotional availability, and other ills, all handicapped me emotionally in my relationships.

MY OTHER FAMILY

I have heard your prayer, I seen your tears; surely I will heal you.
(2 King 20:5)
Love must be without hypocrisy. Detest evil; cling to what is
good. Show family affection to one another with brotherly love.
Outdo one another in showing honor. (Romans 12:9-10)

I had become very anxious about finding my dad, since my mother seemed not to care about me. I always dreamt of meeting him, and wondered how I could find him. I often imagined what if I had a whole other family out there? How would they respond to me if I ever found them? The only information I had was that my father's name was Charles Tolbert, and that he lived in Gary Indiana. I thought about just going through the Gary phone book and call all of the people with the last name of Tolbert, but somewhere down the line I had got distracted from that. There were many times when I would get on my knees and pray to God, that I would find my father and that he would love me, understand me, and what I had been through. Now that I was older, almost forty, I grew from hating God to loving and understanding how He works. As I said earlier, no one ever taught me about the Lord. Most of what I learn was from listening to other people always talking about this man named JESUS! Wondering to myself, who was this person everyone was talking about. *I knew that he would supply all of my needs, and that He will not put no more on me than I could bear*(Phil 4:19; 1 Cor. 10:13).As long as I shall live these two verses will always stick out in my mind.

I began to think of my dad more often, wondering who was he, and what kind of man was he? Did he know that he had a son? Would he accept me or would he hurt my feelings just like everyone else in my life had done? Was my mother right when she would say to me, "What if I did find my father, would he accept me?" I would just continually take my prayers to GOD, asking him if it is in his will that I find my father. Then the Lord blessed me with a son of my own named Brandon, he was born in 1992. That was just like a dream come true because also one of my prayers I would pray is that GOD would bless me with a son, and if he blessed me with a son I would always be there for him. Since that was all I had wanted most of my life, was to be a father and have someone to call me dad.

It would distress me when I would see positive fathers and son relationships, sometimes even seeing how my uncle treated his sons and not me. Believe me there was a differences when it came to my uncle three sons and me. I have to admit there were times while living with my uncle he would address me as his son. I noticed that when he did try to show me any type of affection, it would always be whenever we were not around his wife. That's why I had always felt that she was behind the abuse that I received from my uncle. It was more like he was trying to satisfy her. Talk about a black sheep, that's what they raised me to be and made me feel about myself.

It seemed year after year, rejection after rejection, from my mother, I still prayed and prayed for my dad, until God finally answered my prayers. Of all the people, God used my mother to unite my father and me after almost 40 years of praying. One day while my mother was at work at the Veteran Administration Hospital in Chicago, a man came to the reception desk were she sat and gave his name as Norman Tolbert. My mother asked him, if he had a brother named Charles? Norman hesitated for a moment because he thought that Charles was in some type of trouble. But after the initial shock, Norman told my mother yes, he had a brother name Charles. By the grace of God, my mother's heart was softened to tell Norman to please let Charles know that he has a 39 year old son looking for him. And this is where it all began with *my other family.* My mother gave Norman her phone number so that Charles could call her. He did that same night which was October 26th 1993. Now to show you how GOD works; I was raised all the way up to my teens, thinking that my birthday was October 26th.

Charles and my mother talked and she told him that I had worried her all of my adult life about who was my father and she was so glad she has ran across him. My father Charles decided that he wanted to meet me, so my mother told him she would call me and give me his number. But that is not the way it went, she did not call me first instead she called my very close sister, Pam, and told her the story and asked her to call me. When Pam called me and told me that Dorothy, who is what she had all of her children to call her, she had talked to my father, I thought it was an April fool joke, but I realized that this was the month of October. Pam said, "No I'm not playing. Dorothy really did talk to your father and he wants you to call him." Listening to my sister telling me the story and how it happened I just went numb and dropped to my knees praising God and thanking him for answering my prayers after all these years! I was so emotional, it took me a couple of minutes to regroup and realize that my dreams and prayers had come true; my sister gave me his phone number and told me to call him. I was surprised, astonished, amazed, numb, and in disbelief, and it took me about thirty minutes to get myself together to make the call. This was on a Wednesday night. After about three long rings he answered. I cannot remember all we said to each other that night because I was so overwhelmed. It is just like a big blank to me now. I do remember at the end of the conversation we talked about meeting soon. After talking I found out that my dad lived about four blocks from where I worked. We decide to meet at my job the next day.

Well this was certainly one of those talk show moments; I can remember my dad coming to my job that afternoon with two of my sisters, Carla and Vinnie. Considering all the crying and hugging, my two sisters were in awe of how much I look like our dad! One of my sisters, Vinnie, had a son going to same school where I worked. She said one day her son came home and said that there was a man that worked at his school who looked just like his granddad, but she said she really did not pay him much attention. Of course, because of the family resemblance of me looking just like my father's twin, there was no doubt in their mind that I was my father's son. I was accepted with open arms by my dad's family. We met on a Thursday afternoon, October 27, 1993; just so happened I was having a birthday party for myself the next day Friday, my birthday, October 28th. My new found dad said that he was coming and bringing other family members.

The party went well, even my mother attended. I got a chance for the first time in my life to introduce both my mother and father to my friends. That was the proudest moment of my life. How I had dreamed of being able to see my mother and father in the same place, and to top it off they were both there for me! Even though I had just made forty years old, I felt like I was a little kid all over again, I had the time of my life that night, which I believe I will always remember for the rest of my life.

After the party there was so many question that I had for my dad; I just couldn't ask them all in one day. I can remember not forgetting to thank God every day for finally answering one of my prayers. At this time the holidays were approaching with Thanksgiving being the first one, my dad decided to have Thanksgiving dinner at his house. This is where I got the chance to meet all of my sisters and brother. Oh was that the time of my life, and now after almost a month, I had now *my other family,* six sisters, one brother and a host of nieces, nephews, cousins, aunts and uncles. The good part about it is that everyone accepted me as though I had been in the family all of my life. All I heard that day was how much I look just like my dad. Like I said once I met my other family and my dad, they made me feel so welcome, that after meeting them,

I decide to change both me and my son last names to Tolbert. This really made my dad proud, after meeting him I became his oldest child. Dad said that he had always felt in the back of his mind, that there was a missing piece of the puzzle in his life, which was nothing but God!

To my surprise I saw that my mother seemed to be happy for me also. I think she realized how big of a deal it was for me to find my dad; it was like a weight being lifted off of her. But I also believe that she felt that the past had come back to haunt her. After talking to my dad almost every day, I had the chance to tell him a little about my life. He seemed devastated when I told him that my mother didn't raise me. I told him that I was given up at three months old, and my uncle and his wife raised me through adulthood. I was able to talk about some of the mental and physical abuse that I encountered during my childhood, and he claimed that if he had known that I was born and my mother had given me up, his mother (not him?) would have taken me in. After talking to my dad I found that my mother and he had two different stories of what happened. All I could say is that I do believe that my dad in fact did mentally wound my mother back in those days, because he was a music entertainer at the time and ran across a lot of women. I was his first born. Talking to my mother I could still hear the pain in her voice, and then to top things off, I looked just like Charles. I guess it was too much for her to bear.

I had grown an automatic relationship with my dad, which also helped me to have a better relationship with my children. One thing that I could say is my dad filled that void in my life, it was like I had known him all of my life. It amazed me to find out that even though he was not in my life, we shared some of the same likes and dislikes. I just cannot stop thanking GOD for bringing my dad into my life. I just wish that I could have had him sooner, but I won't complain! By the grace of GOD, I shared sixteen years of my dad's life. My dad is now gone on to be with the Lord; he made his transition April 16, 2009. I am so grateful to GOD that I had the opportunity to see my dad in hospital before he passed. He could not say much, but he gave me a strong hand grip with tears in his eyes, and that was the last time I saw my dad, Charles Tolbert, in this life, but I will see him again!

THE MENDING PROCESS

The lord is my shepherd; I shall not want. He maketh me to lie down in green pastures: he leadeth me beside the still waters. He restoreth my soul: he leadeth me in the paths of righteousness for his name's sake. Yea, though I walk through the valley of the shadow of death, I will fear no evil; for thou art with me; thy rod and thy staff they comfort me. Thou preparest a table before me in the presence of mine enemies; thou anointest my head with oil; my cup runneth over. Surely goodness and mercy shall follow me all the days of my life; and I will dwell in the house of the LORD forever (Psalm 23)

Now that I am fifty four years old, I am continually thankful to God because after what I have been though, He was always there for me. I just love the Lord with all my heart, and I can now say that I know Him better than I have ever known Him before. As I look back over my life, *He has never left me or forsaken me*; *I'm more than a conqueror. I can do all things through Christ who has strengthened me (Det. 31:6; Rom.3:37; Phil 4:13).* I have made it through this life by God's grace and mercy. The word of God tells me that I am a son of God (John 1:12). I know now that there was absolutely nothing I could have done to stop the abuse. I believe that with my whole heart, mind and spirit. I was a helpless victim; the adults in my life had full control, and should assume full RESPONSIBITY!

Occasionally, some of us will block our memories so effectively that they don't surface until many years later. But eventually these memories return, and we may actually have a difficult time believing or trusting our own memories. Often our families will keep the denial system going. If my testimony can help another person not feel alone as I felt, then I have done my job! I believe that one of the healing processes of the victim can also come from helping others. I felt like I was so broken and abused that no amount of glue or bandages, or all the king's horses and all the king's men, could have put me back together again. As a young adult the inner child was still inside of me somewhere; I always hoped that someday the world would be safe for me. By admitting my powerless over the abuse I'm set free today: I realized that it wasn't my fault, (I felt like it was). I've came a long way and still struggle with this; I don't have all of the answers. All I know is that am better and I did not give up. Those life lessons that you learn initially are the hardest to forget, and fortunately or unfortunately traditions pass from one generation to the next. Sometimes we need to change!

Love was something that I was deprived of all my life. So it was very hard for me to show my own children love; it took me years to be able to say I love you and give them a hug. Since I was never taught how to show love, I taught myself. It seemed to me when I did try to love as a child I was pushed away time after time. Eventually it just developed into hate starting with myself, and everybody around me. My history may have shaped me, but it does not define me. By the grace of God I have come a long way. I don't feel uncomfortable anymore hugging a person and telling them I love them—especially my children. What I thought was working against me was actually working for me, and if you can realize that then you can make since out of the pain. Then you justify the pain by saying, *"You know what, it was good for me that I went through this. I'm relieved you didn't stand by me: I'm relieved you left me. I found my way because you left me. I discovered myself when I lost you; I was so engrossed in you that I couldn't see me; the loss of you was discovery of me!"* Now you can celebrate your life and it all begins to make sense (Oprah Winfrey).

As an abused child I didn't have anyone to trust, since the adults in my life were the abusers, I never felt safe. I learned that children have no power over adults, they never have and they still do not. I can clearly see that each setback in my life made me a stronger, wiser, and much better person. I would say that I'm ninety percent healed. I don't know if the remaining ten percent will ever disappear, but always remember, *when you feel like you are in misery don't hold on to it, when misery is breaking loose in your life let it go, and when you are going through misery, keep moving, don't stop!* My past has motivated me to strive to never be in a situation to lose control over my life. I'm still a work in progress.

GET YOUR BREAK THOUGH

Until you heal the wounds of your past, you will continue to bleed–you can bandage bleeding with food, alcohol, drugs, work and sex but eventually it will sting your life, and you will continue would continual to bleed. So you have to find strength to pull out the core of your pain of the memory and make peace with it (Iyanla Vanzant–Oprah Winfrey Show).

You can't embrace your future if you are holding on to your past. You must be able to bring closure to the situation, or else it will bleed over into other situations in your life. Anger does not begin to describe what I felt going through the emotional trauma I did in my life. I felt lost, and my mind was always at war. Every day was a battle for me as a Christian. The devil is a liar and the truth is not in him, I am an over comer! *The Lord says, "Forget what happened before, and do not think about the past. Look at the new thing I am going to do. It is already happening. Don't you see it? I will make a road in the desert and rivers in the dry." (Isaiah 43:18-19).*

We must recognize that operating on our own ego alone will not give us the strength we need and the happiness we deserve. There must be an existing power greater than us, a spiritual reality that can support us in every step of our recovery. To change our negative habits and thought patterns, we need to turn to a power greater than we are. I have tried to change at different periods in my life, only to fall back into my old ways after a short time. With God in my life, and my allowing Him to take an active role in my life, by providing with strength, love, and nurture every day, I was able to change. My life has improved and I have been restored to sanity. It takes a lot of energy to hold on to negatively, or to hold a grudge, and to be angry at people. Even if they have done something horrible to you it only adds pain and frustration, and is damaging to your health and happiness. Maybe be you do not think about it, but the truth is, if you are holding a grudge–*that grudge is really holding you (Oprah Winfrey).* Today it is time to let go. *Take a deep breath and let go!*

Often I would find myself disassociating mentally to a safe place–my own *heaven.* It was something I had to do because if not, I would let my emotions take over me. Thankfully I fought my way back and prayed, and now today I am a strong black attractive blessed brother. I have turned my entire life over to the care of a force totally beyond myself. I could not just turn over some parts and retain others; I had to completely and totally surrender my will and my life over to my higher power. I'm gradually losing my fear, especially my fear of trusting others. I have given control of my life to my Lord and Savior Jesus Christ. I see that trusting God does work, and I can say that I now feel safe and protected. I spent most of my life with my inner child in control. I would look like an adult, but I was really living as though I was still ten, five or even three years old. My inner child had never learned to be happy, and I was constantly trying to find happiness in the wrong places. As a child I thought that I had control, that somehow I was causing the abuse to happen: maybe I was just a bad child. I felt that if I were just obedient, quiet, bright, or whatever it took, this would be enough and the abuse would just stop and I would be safe. I had the feeling that nothing I did was ever good enough. But again today I realize that none of that was true.

In order to repair ourselves, we must realize we are powerless to change the person or persons in our lives who have committed these hideous acts against us. They will never change simply because we want them to change, and they need to find their own salvation. *No matter whom you are what you are going through, or have been through, no matter how hard or difficult life is for you right now, believe me when I tell you, you can make it!* Until now, power and strength was missing from my life; the POWER to be whole and complete as a person, and to have the STRENGTH to be a responsible adult. By God's grace, I have learned how to develop these characteristics, but first I needed to decide where that power was going to come from. Today I truly have a testimony; because of all I have gone through was just for me. It is the word of GOD; *I knew you before I formed you in your mother's womb* (Jeremiah 1:5), and I have no doubt that this message is a true one.

As time went on I began to take tiny baby steps in trust, outside of myself, and deeper into myself. I came to know that all my life, though the good times and bad times, a universal force was keeping me alive so that one day I would become the healthy person I was meant to be. It had to start with my inner-most core; I had to believe it so that my inner-child could finally feel safe. It was time to stop abandoning myself as I believed others had abandoned me. Such things must change no matter what our past. I'm a very good person who has been seriously hurt, and I deserve to have wonderful things happen for me. My Lord and Savior changed the way I felt about myself and changed my attitude toward other people. The Lord has transformed me from victim into a SURVIVOR!

I have been changed from a wounded person to a healthy person, and reprogrammed my thinking so that I could become complete person; I'm now healthy in mind, body, soul and spirit. Although we have to remember when asking GOD to change us, that there is no magic wand to wave over our heads and mysteriously remove all of our defects. There is no fairy dust to cause change, *just plain and simple continual praying is what will do it.* As a young child I would always walk with my head down, but now God has lifted my head up. You may not be able to change what happened to you, but you can change what happens in you. You have to understand that even though the internal situation may be pressing discouragement upon your soul, you have control of your own spirit. You have control over your own attitude, and you have control over you own prayer life. You must understand you have AUTHORTY and you have a CHOICE! *Cheerfully pleasing GOD is the main thing, and that's what we aim to do, regardless of our condition. (2 Corinthians 5:9.)*

The Lord knows that I have stared death in the face many times, from my childhood to adulthood. It began when I was skinned by a truck as I was running after a marble in the streets, to having suicidal thoughts. I was shot at several times and shot once. I have been stabbed, and been the victim of carjacking with a gun pointed to my head with my hands and feet tied up. I was kidnapped, and was in three car accidents, one in which the car I was driving flipped over and slid into oncoming traffic. ***But*** by the Grace of God I'm still here! Somebody was praying for me: God has a destiny for me, and his hands were always over my life. He saved my life so I owe him everything. If it had not been for the Lord on my side I would have been dead a long time ago. I'm giving God all the glory, honor, and praise! God is not though with me yet. Amen!

FORGIVE SO YOU CAN BE FORGIVEN

And when you stand praying, if you hold anything against anyone,
forgive him, so that your father in heaven may forgive you
*your sins (Mark 11:25)*God knew that man needed forgiveness,
so he sent his only son Jesus to deliver all of mankind from
eternal consequences of their sins (1 John 4:9-10)

My testimony is that if I had not gone through what I went though, I would not be in this healthier emotional place. I have a greater capacity for compassion regarding my mother, and this has allowed me to forgive her. And this also goes for the other people in my life that have hurt me through the years. However, I'm still working on forgiveness everyday so I can continue to move forward. *When you forgive a person, it is not about them, it is all about you (T.D. Jakes).* True forgiveness is unconditional: it has no red tape; it has no strings attached. True forgiveness means it's over, and you let go and live on. Forgiveness is not about weakness it is about getting control back over your life; and that you must take AUTHORITY back over your life!

I have learned to forgive those who have trespassed against me. Because my heavenly father has also forgiven me, I know my worth and walk with my head high. I'm on an assignment, and no mission is impossible. *I am purpose driven and destiny focused!* Forgive as the Lord has forgiven you. Jesus not only had the power to forgive, but grant us the ability to forgive others, just as we have been forgiven. Since God for me, who can be against me? (Romans 8:31). I have the author and finisher on my side. God has given me a chance to forgive everyone in my life who has hurt me (including my mother). My uncle and his wife are gone now, but GOD has allowed me to forgive my dad, my uncle and his wife before they made their transition, and each time it felt just like a big weight lifted off of me. *When someone you care about hurts you, you can either hold onto anger, resentment, and thoughts of revenge, or embrace forgiveness and move forward. God will meet you where you are and take you where you need to be.*

Forgiving others may seem to be a choice, and in a sense it is a choice, but GOD has been very clear about forgiveness. He has given us specific direction in numerous scriptures, all of which can be summed up in just one word "FORGIVE!" I believe that GOD is saying that it is in *our own best interest* to forgive; he is not talking about what is the best interest of the person who we need to forgive. We are the ones who GOD is trying to protect; we are the ones who receive the most benefit from forgiveness, not the other person. Also, forgiving others releases us from anger and allows us to receive the healing we so need. The whole reason God has given us specific directions on forgiveness is because he does not want anything to stand between us and him. Forgiving others takes time, and we have a divine example for forgiving others!

At this stage in my life I tried to understand my mother and decided that maybe there was a reason that God allowed me to go through what I went through in my life. Therefore, GOD began putting forgiveness in my heart for my mother. Finally, I had forgiven my mother, and made an effort to have a better relationship with her. I realized as I matured both in age and in Christ, I understood her situation much better, and why she made the decisions she did. I now have grown children and grandchildren, and feel it is important that I be the example of forgiveness God wants me to be. Every day I just thank God for my mother and for giving me the wisdom and understanding that enabled me to forgive her.

It is sad to say that I have done things in my life to hurt other people, and I was not pleasing in God's eyes, but I know that he has forgiven me. I have repented and surrendered my life only to Him. I have accepted what has happen to me, and I have learned not to allow it to ruin or consume my life. When you hold resentment toward another person, you are bound to that person or condition by an emotional link that is stronger than steel. Forgiveness is the only way to dissolve that link and to be free! Release those who have wronged you and go after your destiny.

Now that you know my story, my prayer is that my story will have an impact on your life. You have the ability to turn the pain of today into prosperity for tomorrow. These things came to us to strengthen, empower, and prove to us who we are. This is going to be an uncomfortable journey, but as long as God is traveling with you, there is truly nothing to fear. I feel like I am no longer on auto pilot. I am finally in control. God said it is already done. He is Alpha and Omega–the beginning and the end! He will take the pain away and allow the healing to begin. He is your way through, and your way out!

Bill's Prayer:

> *Father God, I need your help and insight. Today I*
> *have gained a better understanding of forgiving others*
> *and with your help I fully forgive from my heart. Just*
> *as you have freely forgiven me, I forgive them father. I*
> *ask you to forgive me for hurting others out of my own*
> *hurt and to heal my relationship with others. I pray all*
> *of this in JESUS holy and precious name by whom all*
> *forgiveness and healing is made possible. Thank you for*
> *loving me in ways I will never comprehend, in JESUS*
> *name, AMEN!!!*

My passion has led me into my purpose. The Holy Spirit has given me a plan and a purpose. I believe that my true purpose in life is to tell my story. I believe this will help someone who is like I once was. This book is for that person who feels hopeless. I wrote this for those who believe they are unloved, and feel they can do nothing to change their life. But I am here to say there is hope!

JUST DON'T GIVE UP! GOD IS NOT THROUGH WITH YOU YET!

> *Brethren, I do not count myself to have apprehended; but one thing*
> *I do, forgetting those things which are behind and reaching forward*
> *to those things which are ahead, I press toward the goal for the prize*
> *of the upward call of God in Christ Jesus (Philippians 3:13-14)*

The End

Going up
Without the Baggage
GOD says, "The reason
Some people have **turned** against you
And **walked away** from you, without reason,
has **nothing to do with you.** It is because
I have removed them from your life because
They cannot go where I am taking you next.
They will only
Hinder you in
Your **next level,**
Because they
Already served
their purpose
In your life.
Let them go
And
Keep moving.

GREATHER IS COMING"
says the LORD

Pastor David A. Reed

ABOUT THE AUTHOR

I believe God let me go through the things that I did first to trust in him and believe in him and help someone else. It seems like the more I talked about my life story, the more God kept putting it in my heart to write it down. I just continued putting it off until I followed the Holy Spirit and began to cry and write, which took me about a year to get done. I'm presently living in Gary, Indiana, but I was born and raised in Chicago, which I still call home. Once you start this book you will get a better picture of my personal life and how the Holy Spirit moved the pen!